CHANTS FOR THE BEAUTY FEAST

other books by the author

POETRY

Dawn Visions
Burnt Heart/Ode to the War Dead
This Body of Black Light Gone Through the Diamond
The Desert is the Only Way Out
The Chronicles of Akhira
The Blind Beekeeper
Mars & Beyond
Laughing Buddha Weeping Sufi
Salt Prayers
Ramadan Sonnets
Psalms for the Brokenhearted
I Imagine a Lion
Coattails of the Saint
Abdallah Jones and the Disappearing-Dust Caper
Love is a Letter Burning in a High Wind
The Flame of Transformation Turns to Light
Underwater Galaxies
The Music Space
Cooked Oranges
Through Rose Colored Glasses
Like When You Wave at a Train and the Train Hoots Back at You
In the Realm of Neither
The Fire Eater's Lunchbreak
Millennial Prognostications
You Open a Door and it's a Starry Night
Where Death Goes
Shaking the Quicksilver Pool
The Perfect Orchestra
Sparrow on the Prophet's Tomb
A Maddening Disregard for the Passage of Time
Stretched Out on Amethysts
Invention of the Wheel
Sparks off the Main Strike
Chants for the Beauty Feast

THEATER / THE FLOATING LOTUS MAGIC OPERA COMPANY

The Walls Are Running Blood
Bliss Apocalypse

PROSE

Zen Rock Gardening
The Little Book of Zen
Zen Wisdom

CHANTS FOR THE BEAUTY FEAST

poems

June 3 – October 28, 1997

Daniel Abdal-Hayy Moore

The Ecstatic Exchange
2011
Philadelphia

Chants for the Beauty Feast
Copyright © 2011 Daniel Abdal-Hayy Moore
All rights reserved.
Printed in the United States of America

For quotes any longer than those for critical articles and reviews, contact:
The Ecstatic Exchange,
6470 Morris Park Road, Philadelphia, PA 19151-2403
email: abdalhayy@danielmoorepoetry.com

First Edition
ISBN: 978-0-578-07482-5 (paper)

Published by *The Ecstatic Exchange*,
6470 Morris Park Road, Philadelphia, PA 19151-2403

Also available from The Ecstatic Exchange:
Knocking from Inside, poems by Tiel Aisha Ansari

Cover collage by the author
Back cover photograph by Malika Moore
Text originally designed by Ian Whiteman

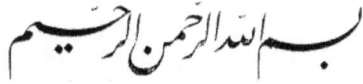

DEDICATION

To
Shaykh ibn al-Habib
(and the continuation of the Habibiyya)
Shaykh Bawa Muhaiyuddeen,
all shuyukh of instruction and ma'arifa
and to
Baji Tayyaba Khanum
of the unsounded depths

---

*The earth is not bereft
of Light*

CONTENTS

Picture of the Garden   9
Flower Shapes   10
Correspondences   12
The Story of the Czechoslovakian Button-Maker   14
Goldfish   17
Half-Circle of Light   19
Heartbeat of the Skies   21
Ordering Chinese   23
Dappled Place   25
Forgiveness   28
Funeral   30
Spinning Top   32
Story of the Woman Whose Head was a Rosebush   34
Winding Green Tendril   36
He Wrote on the Walls   39
Happiness   42
Musical Instrument   45
The Ecstatic Drinker   48
Placement   50
The Story of the Blind Landscape Architect   52
A State of Love   55
A Very Small White Horse   58
Heartburst   62
A Blue Leaf   64
Head Without Images   66
Boy on Bicycle   68
TWA Flight to Albuquerque   70
Clouds   72
Falling Asleep in an Airplane above the Clouds   74

Head of a Pin   76
The Divine Order   78
I'd Forgot upon Waking   81
The Book of Roses   83
The Unknown Quandaries of Fate   87
Why Isn't the Air Filled with Singing?   89
Things People Leave Behind   90
When Facing a Dragon   92
Another Life   95
The New York Philharmonic on TV Playing Brahms' First
    Symphony   99
Inventory   103
A Place Not Unlike Pittsburgh   106
Gunshot or Backfire   108
On a Shoestring   111
Name of God   112
The Soul   117
New Physics   120
Guest Speaker   123
Totally Unique   125
Post Traumatic Stress   129
Lost and Found   131
Kick a Blue Ball   133
Theft in a Foreign Country   135
Not For Sale   140
The Beauty Feast   142

Index of Titles   146

The eye of man hath not heard, the ear of man hath not seen, man's hand is not able to taste, his tongue to conceive, nor his heart to report, what my dream was.
— Bottom (from Shakespeare's *A Midsummer Night's Dream*)

We are soulful gardeners
tending the bushes of the King
pruning circumstantial rose trees
waiting for the perfect bloom
— from *Halley's Comet,* by the author)

PICTURE OF THE GARDEN

There is a picture of The Garden
  as a garden within a garden
(by which I mean Paradise),

one state enclosed by another state,
one embrace folded in the
   loving arms of another, greater,
     deeper, greener,

more far-reaching, with
heavenly valleys, gorges, golden
   sunlight everywhere,

laughing children, rare

flowers.

6/3

FLOWER SHAPES

Flowers in the shapes of cozy houses,
   fountains in the shapes of windows
     opening onto gardens,
roadways over bridges in the shape of
   prancing white horses,
bridges leaping over gurgling streams in the

shape of two people in love gazing into
   each other's eyes over
     tea and cucumber sandwiches,

esplanades in the shape of classical German literature,

trees flying upward like stationary flames,
   their dark leaves rippling endlessly upward
in the shapes of deep-sea tropical lantern fish
suddenly become Flamenco dancers on a
   hot Spanish night in Granada,

the garden itself in the shape of a heartbeat
all alone over the edge of the world, face
   to the black night,

the black night itself in the shape of a
   garden circling endlessly back
     into itself like
       circulating blood,

eyes and faces of children from the subcontinent

or from Madagascar, surrounded by
    exotic vegetation,

the moment in which the garden is glimpsed
in the shape of all those missed opportunities
or in the shape of a sudden breakthrough in the
    heart,

the heart of the garden, the voice of the
   garden in the shape of an
angel's wing that opens onto a
    stairway within a stairway within a
      stairway that leads either

up or down depending on your
   preference, or where your

garden-shaped, fire-shod feet have led you in
this life.

                                                            6/8

CORRESPONDENCES

Not all the flowers have human faces,
not all the flowers speak with human voices.
There isn't an absolute correspondence
    between our souls and
every growing, creeping thing in the garden.
Not every ant approaches with the
    deepest familiarity, each sunbeam that
falls at our feet or on our faces
      doesn't whisper a phrase of wisdom in
        elegant language familiar to
the ears of our souls. The

sound of falling is foreign to us, the
    sound of collapse, even though the
anchor of gravity pulls everything
down. But even in the greatest

variety of twitching and shivering consciousness
of everything going its way with
    creaturely determination, we all,
facing in all directions, recognize in
each other the slavehood of everything at once
to the Noble Creator of all of us at once,
in our eyes, in our voices, the

voices of trees in the wind, the *shush* of
  water on shore, seabirds
dipping and screaming at sunset, the
sunset itself with its red fever and then

      its blue chill, the

night itself with its transparency
      pulled down over all,
pinpoints of galaxies full of explosions and
      planets with their own
           orbiting moons
shining above us as tiny star-pricks in the
skin of the dark,

the whole creation itself turning its
pure soul Creatorward.

                                                  6/14

THE STORY OF THE CZECHOSLOVAKIAN BUTTON-MAKER

This is the story of the Czechoslovakian
   button-maker, whose family fled an
army of caparisoned, black-booted, saber-swinging
    musket-blowing soldiers, young men with
ruddy faces and puffing cheeks, scared
   shitless themselves in all their
      flounce and pomp, and the nobleman

young button-maker-to-be and his father and
mother and two sisters and three brothers and
servants, maids and two black
   Labrador retrievers fled a
mansion on a hill, room after
    room of crystal chandeliers and
beveled mirrors mathematically
     multiplying the magnificence,

and terrace after terrace of formal gardens with
   wild plots you got to through bushes,
birds in almost constant archways of
    dazzling flight, tall banks of black
cypress trees, an actual
   river whose sound was always
     discernible wherever you
stood, inside the house or
   out, gardens, white
rose gardens, gardenia walls, walnut
trees, trellises of morning glories,

they fled in the night with their
belongings in bundles on hay-carts pulled
    by the servants
        lumbering along, but the

boy couldn't say farewell to his beloved
gardens, couldn't glimpse for the last time
the enchanted enclosures.

Years in sooty cities passed, two flights
    up, schoolrooms, back rooms,
the family in poverty, then in
        passing gentility, then he

grew older and found his métier, carving
ivory buttons for the local shirt maker.
Round, oblong, square, diamond-shaped
    buttons out of ivory, but

unbeknownst to the wearers of the
elegant shirts, behind each button
he'd carved, so small you couldn't
    see it except under a magnifying
glass, a portion of his childhood
gardens remembered, a corner, a
    sunny glade, a passage between
hedges, a lake with sudden
sunlight, a rosebush
    in bloom, a-hum
with bee music. Carved so

gently into the ivory you'd say there was
nothing there at all

but smooth bone.

6/17

GOLDFISH

Goldfish float in a watery element
in which rise also green ribbony
tendrils wavering fetchingly in the
up-currents. But often these

little glittering dynamos just
hang suspended in water like a
thought or an afterthought, then
turn their noses and
    dart away.

Their faces show no emotion. We
can't be sure of the
emotional life of goldfish, Walt Disney
    notwithstanding. Their

faces are poker faces, impassive, almost
cruel. Saucer eyes, down-turned
    mouths, no emotion.

Yet they are full of desire. They are
desires with two fins and a tail, darting
forward in water or
floating there awhile just before darting.
They lunge toward food. Or in the
    wild, often to their
detriment, toward something
    gleaming.
In the Honolulu airport between planes

I strolled in a little airport garden
and came upon an arched Japanese bridge and
    picture-perfect pond full of
gorgeous multicolored *koi* fish shining
    iridescent in the hot Hawaiian sun.

I was eating a bag of corn chips, and casually
tossed a few into the pond just to
    see what would happen.

Suddenly the *koi* came together
in a kind of thrashing rainbow knot, jutting their
O-shaped pouty lips above water and
snapping the corn chips up with a great
sound of crunching.
I tossed in some more and listened as they
    noisily crunched.

I was transfixed by the sound of these
serene silent *koi* snapping up corn chips,
the sight of them fighting in the water,
and the amazingly loud cracking sound of them
snapping them in their mouths
has never left me, popping sounds like
hundreds of firecrackers going off,

the rhythmically syncopated
clattering sound of gorgeous
golden *koi* in Hawaii

crunching corn chips!

                                                6/17

HALF-CIRCLE OF LIGHT

I've decided never to sleep again.

I'm staying awake forever under that
    jasmine tree over there,
trailing my hand in meandering
    turquoise waters while herons take
        off and land all around me,

and when my eyelids get heavy and go
    down like tenement Venetian blinds in
New York humid summers, and the world wants to
curl up asleep inside my head and turn off all
    extraneous outside noise with an
absolute twist of the sleep knob, I'll

play my glass trumpet of awakened energy until
birds fall out of the trees, the sun rises at
    midnight, wheels turn square and
        burst into flame,

I'll sing snatches of old Mongolian threshing tunes,
    catch the
drift of ancient Japanese metaphysical
arguments over Gō boards, carve
    the sibyl's answers
on a single jade leaf and attach it to an
extraterrestrial spindly coral tree so it
    reflects off the
silvery waters of distant planetary lakes.

There's no time for hesitation. I'll
never go to sleep again.

I'll walk in hobo shoes until I reach the
   speed of freight trains, wave my
arms across train trestles, conduct
shadows like a symphony across crags of
   Colorado canyons,

but I'm actually falling asleep right now
in the midst of writing this poem, so I'll

have to tunnel through to tomorrow with only a
thin thread of consciousness, light making a half-
circle at the far end of the
   dark length of night

I'll soon be asleep in.

6/18

HEARTBEAT OF THE SKIES

A great summer thunderstorm
   bellowed through the house tonight,
long sonic tubas of thunder
    momentarily snaking into
the air of our rooms and
   shaking us to our foundations, our

black cat, low to the ground, streaking
across the floor and down the
stairs to hide in the basement and be
safe from what fills the air like a
   pregnant pause, like a balloon filled
to the brim, like a radiation
     no one's safe from.

It came not with bells but with drum-rolls.

It swirled in on muddy green eddies.

The sky closed in all around the
   house like a tea cozy,
then punched the oxygen full of symphonic
     expansion. Humid and fragrant.
Thrilling and vibrant.
An ecstasy of elasticity and
   sudden zeal.

An after-rumble seemed to subside all around it,
the storm having opened up our pores

to an expression of mercy translated into
a language of light in a lightning bolt, the
    classical solemnity of
Godly proclamation in a thunderclap.

Silence turned inside out
to catch the falling Godly drops.

Our ears turned inside out
to catch the heartbeat of the skies.

                                                   6/18

ORDERING CHINESE

I've ordered out for Chinese
and I gave the address very slowly to
   a man whose English seems
       choppy at best,
then repeated it again very slowly

and now I'm worried the driver, maybe a
   moon-faced teenager or a
very old long-beard Taoist, will get lost
on the way, maybe go up some
    labyrinthine byway, ending up in the
forest at the end of our street, feeding the
shrimp with garlic curry to some
snaky denizen of the woods, or a bevy of
   hungry beetles in the grass, or turn a

corner into time-warp and end up in a
palace courtyard surrounded by
dragon statues, or in the cliff-side hut of
  one of the
lesser ministers in exile from
    court life writing his
memoirs, penning elegant poems
lamenting the passing of the
   Golden Age, ponds with bruised white
petals landing on them,
twitching in the wind, spinning
    slowly on a surface of
black water.

But actually a lithe and able-bodied young
    man of about thirty, calls in at the
screen door in a matter of minutes,
    smiling, hands me the food nice and
hot in a brown paper bag, turns and goes

back to the night-dark street and
drives away.

                                              6/20

DAPPLED PLACE

A spot of light in a dappled place
   outlining leaf forms and petal forms
and fantastical flowers, some in the
   shape of flowers and
some in the shape of elaborate architecture
or the lives of the saints.

Sound is important. Like the
   background, the enlightened background
noise right now outside in the
   dawn dark of awakening birds who
seem to celebrate the mere fact of
waking with the densest chorus, layer upon
   layer, of repeated cheeps and
     chortles, O if

only we could sing out such glad praises upon
   waking! Create a
patchwork of heartfelt song in the air like a
dense arbor of vines and sonic tendrils
winding and weaving in the
   increasing sunlight, a slate
blue right now between the
silhouette black of tree branches and
bush twigs —

the dappled place far inside the heart-mind,
some lakes there and various
   serene bodies of water,

steps of water, Cambodian type terraces of
   irrigation troughs,
      occasional lotuses.

Everything reaching out from inside to
manifest in as brilliant and
  beautiful way as possible
under the circumstances, the
  circumstances being the
miraculous leafiness of the
   gardens of the heart in the
first place, with sly
  animal faces appearing and
     disappearing among their
leaves and level
   places.

And a serene silence in
movements, as in the
movements of growing, the
mysterious consciousness of green

plant-end knowing where to go, reaching out for
warm light and growing to there,
knowing where to twine around and where to
hold onto, as the

Morning Glory plants do in my
back garden tendriling around the
black metal remnant of basketball
  backboard pole

this very moment, putting out tentative

   green feelers, bursting into
      absolute flower!

                                                 6/21

FORGIVENESS

Forgiveness is a doorway of light in a
   dark building in the
     worst part of town,

it's a globule of nectar dripped
   down from an exotic flower that
blooms only once each year on an
     ice-glittery Himalayan peak,

it's a herd of new lambs appearing
   miraculously to a nomadic tribe
     suffering from drought.

Forgiveness is a victim's mother
looking into the eyes of the accused and saying,
"The sky is so blue, every tiny forget-me-not
     is bathed in its light."

Forgiveness is the current in the
   electric chair turning into
     choirs of angels, singing a
   single high note celestially
       over and over.

Forgiveness is the prodigal son or daughter
   returning home to the agéd parents
     with scars and beatitudes
and not a word spoken of the disappearance —
the table is set, the steaming

    food set down, the
        glasses filled.

Forgiveness is a field of wildflowers
    burst into bloom like flames,
illuminating the face of the estranged,
it's the sound of tubas at the
    bottom of a well, the
sound of a beloved's voice after years of strife,

it's a neon Yes after blackout nights of No,
it's the heart weeping a thousand
    years of tears until the
  exhausted body around it
      is renewed, gets up,

turns on a faucet whose running water
whispers, *"I forgive you,"*
the tears are brushed back and
the face becomes the
    face of the full moon,
bright saffron in the night

in the heat of a Philadelphia summer

    bathed in quiet.

6/22

FUNERAL

In memory of my mother-in-law, Roz Goldman

After the funeral, everyone goes home.
But the dead person goes into the ground.

The coffin is closed. The straps are lowered.
People place roses on the lid and some trowelfuls of dirt.
A moment of silence as the canvas straps squeak against
   their metal rods.
The coffin is lowered into the ground.
As the lid disappears, people start chatting under the
     canopy in the afternoon sun: *"So, how's college?"*
        "How're the kids?" "Have you
seen Uncle Charlie?"
But the dead person goes into the ground.

There's one person missing from the conversations.
Her lips are sealed.
Her eyes are closed.

The dead person goes into the ground
as the people leave in their cars, hug and
   commiserate, weep a little, feel an
      emptiness.
One goes back to New York to penthouse
or back to college dorm with its
   dirty socks and microwave.
But the dead person goes into the ground.

The soul of the dead person sees it all, hears
all the remarks, the eulogies and apologies.
The soul hopes to be loved, and loves with
    the essence of love itself,
each powdered face, each neck with knotted necktie,
each grandchild and cousin,
as the body is lowered into the earth
by the people who've been left living up above
    by the side of the grave, who

turn to go with memory pictures flickering, a
    smile from the deceased, a few
fragile words from a few years ago,
events and benefits received from her hands or heart,
eccentricities noted, annoyances
        forgotten.

They get into their cars and drive away
and go home
as the dead person is lowered into the ground.

But while they're not looking *(though*
   even if they did they'd
     see nothing)
the dead person also goes home, to the soft
   sound of a shift in space, a door opening,
a salutation.

By different routes

all going home.

                                             6/24

SPINNING TOP

Somewhere a little top the color of ash
   is spinning. Is it on the

bald forehead of the astronomer-explorer
who saw as plain as day that the
entire cosmos was shaped like a perfect
   figure eight with
      nothing beyond it or
within it other than
      itself?

Or does the top spin
   along the burning edge of a colossal
heavenly body moving through space like the
soporific denizen of a summer beach in
   New Jersey whose walrus
     bulk just lies there as the
sand drifts around it — in this
     case, *stars*?

This top, this spinning entity, is it
the human heart, the *qalb*, whose name in Arabic
   means *"to turn around, overturn,*
     transform, transmute,"

or was it merely the intro into this
poem and had no other function than to open the
   inner eyes like a couple of drowned sailors
     suddenly come back to life,

eager to tell the incredible stories each
    of them has to tell
(bare-breasted South Sea Islanders
    brown as coconuts,
  laughter down by wharfs late at
    night, weird
  lantern lights over rippling black
    water just before dawn,
harrowing narrow escapes)

and as the top whizzes faster, the
tales get more fantastic, until the

top all but disappears completely,
and, as in all images in this world,

we're left with nothing

but the spinning.

6/26

STORY OF THE WOMAN WHOSE HEAD WAS A ROSEBUSH

There's the story of the woman whose
    head was a rosebush, whose
fingers were ferns, whose feet were
    transient roots able to
uproot and root again anywhere in an
    instant. She had
begonia eyes and a mouth of shell,
her belly was moss-covered earth.
Her legs were trees, birch, slender,
    shapely, wobbly, wind-blown,
        supple, unbranched,
made rustling sounds when moving, her

hands were a mountain of ferns rotating their
finger-fronds in the evening breeze, they were
caressing and soft and green, they
touched soft baby skin with an
    equal and appropriate softness.

Her womb was deep and odorous, little
    rootlets hung down in it,
it resounded like a cavern where the
    essential nature of nature is trapped,
whose tension of energy energizes
    the fructification of seeds and their
        eventual sprouting.

Her face was full of the features of leaves, leaves

of all kinds and from all kinds of geographies.
Her lips were of shell. Upon that

translucent pearl green and pearl blue
    luster small petals lay,
brought to life by her words of the
    beginning of cycles, laments for the
ends of seasons and the cold death that
precedes rebirth in an always
        expanding realm.

Her arms lay on the tabletop in the kitchen
like inert presences, like
vines that seek handhold,

like trusting extensions into
beneficent air.

Her heart resounded with that
silence that pervades vast expanses of
nature, open stretches, deserts, buttes,

sky at one with the earth beneath it,

that always astonished look in the eyes of the sky
her unflinching gaze.

6/28

WINDING GREEN TENDRIL

A winding green tendril moves along the
   ground like an electric cord, twists and
turns through short grass and
flowers into a grand piano!

A straggly root pushes down through gravelly soil
in the dark, in thick earth, unsure of
   what to expect, and
bursts through the ceiling of a parking garage!

Hillsides filled with multicolored wild flowers
suddenly burst into twelve part harmony
in broad daylight!

"Unexpected surprises await us," says the
Jolly Green Giant leaning his back against
Half Dome, dabbling his feet in the
   Merced. He says that phrase in a
normal, almost nonchalant, conversational
tone, but the winds pick it up, amplify it,
set it to music, and when it
rolls into Las Vegas it's wearing
   spangle tuxedos and doing
precision dance steps in the manner of
James Brown, the hardest working
   tendril in show business.

A somber light stretches out across Alaska.

This extravaganza costume picture
    rolls backwards, and all the
racial migrations to the
    North American continent are
visible in their backwards chronological
  order, Africans then
    Europeans then Native Americans then
Europeans then Arabs then Africans then smatterings of
Vikings and Mongols and Hairy Ainu and
Cro-Magnon aunt Grognik who shows how to sew together
    skins, and her husband
      uncle Snok who
shapes flint arrowheads by mathematically
precise rock-striking methods that take
three days of deep calculation and prayer.

A songbird in the night expresses things
    human beings only think. If
human beings could only sing like this bird sings
war would be no more.

"But we are what we are,"
says the Green Giant, less jolly in the
   fading light, picking out a
suitable club from the many fallen tree boughs
    littering the little valley.
"You can never be too prepared for danger,"
he intones wisely as the
    dark envelopes him.

Some delicate black buds, unbeknownst to the others,

open in the night, and gulp in the
    cool night air, ecstatic.

A firefly beeps official firefly Morse Code to its nearby firefly lover:

blink-blink-blink-blink / black.
blink-blink / black.

blink-blink-blink-blink / black.
blink-blink / black.

                                                                7/1

HE WROTE ON THE WALLS

He wrote on the walls, he wrote on the
   ceiling, he
wrote on trees, he wrote meticulously
   on the bark over each little
     crevice and rough spot until the
entire tree was covered with his writing,

he wrote on water, on blinking
currents, on thin places where
water slides over rocks,

he wrote on moving things, on
small mammals underground, babies of
mouse or mole family suckling at their
   mothers' pink teets, he'd
cover their fur and even their
little wizened earnest mammal faces with
    writing,

he couldn't stop, each slender grass blade has his
writing on it, each bulbous
    cloud,

he almost never lifted his pen from his
   writing, so
driven was he to write,

across warm human bodies, even
   across the dead, he wrote

    that particular unified look on the
       faces of the dead, unified with
          death itself and
somehow finally unified with each other, each
       other face in
         entire humanity, he
wrote that, he perfected the technique,

he was a daring writer, he took
chances and made gigantic
leaps in space as well as
gigantic leaps of faith,

the garden virtually sparkled with his
    writing, the impeccable
       grammar, the
          excited imagery, the
perfect rhymes,
his indelible trademark flourishes and
unmistakable characteristics, of
    his and no other
       authorship, his

writing that we always are
reading in mid-sentence, since he's
never done and always so tireless, we'll
    never get to the end, and
try as we might, even inching closer and
    closer, never
get all the way back to the beginning, to that
first time his pen hit a surface and

started writing, even though

somehow we catch a glimpse of the
beginning in a leaping
rainbow trout at dusk on
   gray-green lake water,

in gleams of light in window panes covered
with his writing at the
crack of dawn, in the middle of the dark,
the first bird that sings its chorus at the
   first tweak of light,

we almost get the moment of beginning at those
tiny pauses where he dipped
   pen in ink before
     continuing writing,
we almost get his initial
heartfelt impulse

in the midst of such voluminous writing.

7/6

HAPPINESS

I think I might be happiest if I
   woke up in the morning facing a
     bright blue sea, fishermen in the
morning light throwing out their nets, water
   sloshing up around my boat, and I could

spend the early morning looking out, up on one
   elbow, sniffing sea air.

Or I might be just as happy waking on a
teak platform under a rainforest canopy, giant
   ferns crossing their sunlit latticework
     above me, macaws
screaming in the distance, chattering and
   dove-piping, slow peaceful
     slosh of waterfall
       constantly by my ear.

We're turned inside out by sleep.
We wake in the opposite direction from where we
   went to sleep in the night,
a great sweet horse face with long
   eyelashes looking down at us
in the deep forest, waiting to take us for a
warm morning swim.

The day turns us right-side out again until
night time. Then we

snuggle back in time and space —
but I'd be happiest

waking up miles from where I slept, so far
I couldn't even see that
distant position, guarded over by
pure grace, sipping from that

    pool.

2

And three hours later, when I
do wake up, the very

first thing is the song of the
mockingbird gloriously syrupy clear and

bright to itself in the
faint dark, then I

put on the body, heavy length, and
need to pee, the centralized

strain of it, then remember
the first part of this poem and

think, challenged, I must write a
second part, facts, direct sensory, nothing

fancy at 5 a.m. in the exact same
Philadelphia I fell asleep in except that

now it's quiet and endless and that
bird's majestic selfhood opening itself

out before its Lord in song

I can't sing, nor can

any ant.

7/6-7

MUSICAL INSTRUMENT

Here's an extra long musical instrument, it has
thousands of stops, a bell that
   opens out like a brass calla lily,
tubing that coils like Medusa's hairdo,
   you pour water through one end and
listen to its deep pipes gurgle,
you depress those buttons at the other end for
    explosive chords in a
minor key.

Use this instrument to accompany
the inauguration of gunboats, the
   burning down of a house with
     all your belongings in it,
the marriage of a soprano
   to a blind saxophonist.

It's also splendid for theatrical performances
   where lots of Corinthian columns topple
onto toga-and-gray-suit wearing chattering
    politicians, or
set up by the side of the sea
to warn boats of treacherous shoals
or swimmers of treacherous boats.

It's an instrument unlike any other,
it emits sounds to make a plague of locusts
shiver in their boots, the
   final notes of a piano concerto

hang in the air like the sword of Damocles
    swinging over the audience's heads.

Yet some dulcet tones coaxed from its
    more delicate grille work can still
enchant the tyrannical czar and his royal
    family seated on a rooftop in a picture-pose
awaiting execution *(one escapes to become
    a men's magazine centerfold)*,
or the high hum of coordinated
    breathing and imagining —
intake of breath, press a note, hear the
squeeze box throb, imagine your
childhood vacation spot, the
Jersey Shore, Lake Tahoe in those
extra-baggy swim trunks of the yawning 50s.

But there's a time when everyone sits around it
and plays a portion of the Great Melody
on whatever portion of the instrument they're near.

The miracle is that lament and dirge and
mournful song are played at the same time as
jubilation and gospel get-down shouts and
happy crescendos rising like whales spouting,
all differing and contradictory moods played
simultaneously like sheets of glass
slid across each other, showing
the many minute temperaments of naked mankind,

and through it all you can hear a

single melody that no one alone can hum, and
when people stop playing their portion
this melody disappears
like a willowy shadow cast on a vaporous wall,
and only emerges when the people are all
    together again playing.

The curtain goes up on a life
to the sound of this instrument, like
   florid accompaniment to a
     silent movie.

The curtain goes down on a life
to the silence of this instrument, and
then that thin melody emerges with the
force of ten tropical hurricanes of
beneficent choir harmonies in an
    elusive dimension
come to life on the lips of an iridescent
   angelic powerlessness so

profound as to excite chords never
   heard on this earth, beyond all

earthly powers of imitation.

7/17

THE ECSTATIC DRINKER

Sober, the ecstatic drinker
throws his glass into the lake
and the entire garden is
reflected in its open oval,
lights as if from nighttime fireflies
float up the glass's sides,
and into its cavity all the
lake's waters flow until he
finds himself standing in a
dry crater, the
full moon of his own
face no longer reflected
on the shimmer of its
    surface.

Shocked, he shakes the
glass, tries to pour the
lake waters out, but the
now sober glass remains adamant,
all that lovely water
trapped inside.

He feels desolate.
He sits down and sings a song.
The song invites all the
flowing things of the
universe to a rhythmic dance, ecstatic
  obedience
to their Creator, trees to

   fling their hair, flames to
turn cylindrical,
stars to join in
whirling circles around a
still center, and he
stands up himself and
throws back his head in song which is
rippling laughter, and a parallel

clap of laughter
rushes to his center from the
circling trees and hills, the
waters of the lake he
finds himself inside of rising
inside and around him,
the full moon of his
face illuminating the
late flight of herons to their
nests, their long
cries echoing across the
bright blue waters, the clear

glass of his
heart filling to its
open oval and
overflowing over and over as it

drinks and sings.

7/21

PLACEMENT

> *"Allah sends some to the Garden and some to the Fire, and He does not care."*
> — Tradition of the Prophet Muhammad,
> peace and blessings of Allah be upon him

Oh Allah, You place us where You will.
In a room on the 18th floor of a
   Days Inn in Chicago overlooking
year 2000 concrete buildings rocketing
     skyward, some windows lit, some
windows dark on
   cubicles humans live and work in
at 4 a.m. in the morning, the mauve heavens
      brightening.

Or You place us on
cool mountaintops among huge cork trees in
   northern Morocco rugged
     as stones, like Shaykh ibn Mashish,
head the entire sky from horizon to horizon,
   who, when he invoked Allah, the
      whole mountain shook.

Or You place us in the
deep cramped holds of slave ships, body
chained to body, dark, damp,
deathly, to a strange country and
   forced in servitude to do
     work we've never done before,
and whipped if we waver.

Oh Allah, You do this, in
   Your wisdom, Your
      sweet dominion.
You put wings on butterflies and take the
legs off snakes, and they
   slither away.

You bring to life the criminal and the saint
out of the same womb if necessary

and head us toward You

and display the world to our faces,
and give us words to name the
world we're in the way You
gave them to Adam.

Garden or Fire, *and You do not care.*

And Your Mercy
everywhere.

7/25

THE STORY OF THE BLIND LANDSCAPE ARCHITECT

> *"The door to the invisible
> must be visible"* —
> — René Daumal

This is the story of the blind landscape architect
who designed everything from inner vision,
who saw spatial relationships between the
    shadows and lights of his heart,
who sat at great sheets of art paper with
stubs of charcoal and pencil in his
    hands, and drew out the
winding paths, elevated mounds, dips, crests of
land, scribbled-in streams, bridges,
clumps of trees, clusters of bushes, rows of
flower beds, indicated
    purples and blues and lavenders,
fuchsia pink and hibiscus red,
water fountains where a
    loop of water would arc into the
air then shut off at the source so the
arc of water would be
    suddenly cut off in space and arch its
top loop and then come sliding down into the
pool with a series of delicate
    sibilant plops.

He let his hands flow across the sheets only a
few inches above the paper, then circle with a

pencil to indicate wild areas and
tame areas, areas with white
    peacocks and a cockatoo or two,
and if the garden is big enough, areas of a
small herd of miniature deer, tame, and
    not too ravenous.

He stood up from his
    drawing board and
turned to face the very place he'd designed with its
breezes and mint smells, he'd
walk the small paths he'd creatively foreseen,
sat by the fountain and heard the lazy
plops of the water's trajectory back into
    the flat water of the pool.

The garden flourished in the visible
whose source was the invisible.

Its leaves and buds protruded into the
visible from the musky richness of the deep
invisible realm.

He turned and walked through to the
    other side. His
blindness linked him to the goal of all
    sight, the winding
paths, little arched
    bridges over fresh streams,
sounds of praising birds in branches of
    insubstantial trees,

momentary song holding sweet melody in
    air before looping in air
then sliding down into deep silence.

Drops of water on each leaf. Bright
glisten-dots from the source of all
   light seeming to
     look at us as we
pass.

Fluffy, serrated, multiform petals and
delicate imaginary shapes of flowers
turning us like their own budding offspring
to face the calm face of wonder in this

visionary garden
of perfect vision.

                                                  7/28

A STATE OF LOVE

A state of love so total
raspberry vines intertwined with dark
   lagoon shadows, splashes of
light so bright they make everything else
     silhouette.

A state of love so total
nothing remains of the lover, only a
   few pale threads, they
too soon gone, ignited in air like
sparklers, fizzy with sparks, incandescent
white centers, splatterings of a goldener
brightness around a hundred central halos,
so deep has the lover gone
spacelessly into the Beloved,

the air like a vibrating string, twanging
back and forth in the compass of its
arc so fast it can't be seen, and
has to be heard. And what's
   heard is so deep

   underground seismic groans don't begin to
match it, skies colossal with thunderclouds
don't begin to intimate the utter
sweeping majesty of it, water and
   sky mixed in a huge tumult of
waves of electrified
tides and zigzag lightning don't even

    come close to the
grandness of it,

a love so deep and so total and so self-
abnegating, so self-
  voiding, so emptying of the
usual familiar bacterial
    specimens from our lakes, habits,
quirks, deep-down anguish and
    neuroses, holding on for
dear life, for
  fear of death, yet

death is the great insider to all our
   outside wondering, it's the great
spreading out into a wider expanse after all this
life's tweedling narrowness and
   frustrated oppressiveness, it's the
great opening onto pure openness,

onto a love so total and so
deep even silence betrays what it's like, since it's

actually no different from the textured sensation of the
    present moment,

God's Voice of Compassion
coming down into us through the heart valve

like a fall of ignited white roses, tips
  flecked with blood, tumbling

petals-first into our

usual gray domains.

                                          7/30 (57 years old today)

A VERY SMALL WHITE HORSE

A very small white horse
   saunters over to the lip of a clear
     pool, dips its head and
sips the water
in a vast bronze desert landscape
with bright turquoise sky

on a postcard held by the fingers and
   thumb of a right hand
belonging to a child in a grand ballroom with
crystal chandeliers and oriental carpets
filled with hushed activity, the
   comings and goings of servants and
foreign diplomats, a glimpse of the
Swiss Alps out a
   distant window

in a book illustration held in the lap of a
young turbaned student from India
peering through round spectacles at the
very large book with quizzical intent
going fifty miles an hour on the
Orient Express in a very posh upholstered
overstuffed chair in the
drawing room

all of which has been meticulously watercolored by
the Orient Express architect named Bosian whose picture
of this scene sits face up on his top shelf as he

draws at a drawing board in a
   circle of light on the
top floor of a high rise building in
   London, pipe smoke billowing,
sketching kaleidoscope patterns for a
   series of gardens planned for the
royal apartments, a fly lands on the
   page he's drawing on, he plops an
empty jam jar upside-down over it to
   trap it, seen through the

binoculars of a rival architect in the
   office opposite named
Abercrombie, whose daughter in white
flounces is whining about pastry and
   pulling at his jacket

on the movie poster for the new
murder mystery at the Strand entitled
"The Architect's Demonic Daughter,"
the large block print title on the poster

still visible from a distance down the
foggy London Street on the double-decker red
   bus wheezing as it
     swooshes past in a corner of the

movie frame in which a very white, tall American
   woman in willowy blue dress is
talking in sultry tones to a black detective with
square jaw in a restaurant lighted by a

single yellow candle flame that
casts a nimbus glow on the

face of the reader reading this poem or
the listener listening to this poem being
    read out loud
in a landscape of furniture or trees
inside a house or outside in the
   open somewhere
in an almost visible atmosphere, like a
greenish mist, of intellectual, imaginal
   innermost focus, a subtlety
     palpable even from the

next world where
thought-forms and spirit-forms
view the entire proceedings of creation from a
safe distance, not in the
   clouds, but in another

dimension altogether that curiously
    intersects ours, on a

mountaintop, on a planet in space, in an
engulfing wave of all possible
animation like the silken rainbow-
   colored oily skin that
    swirls across the watery
surface of a bubble

turning ever-so-slowly above a

Throne not-of-this-world at all,

a Throne that is not even a
    throne, in which
our awe and bewilderment, in love's
    elegant light,

become speechless at last.

                                        8/2-3

HEARTBURST

I feel my heart's about to burst
(too much tea, too much coffee ice cream?)
but what will it burst into?

Will it be just a
   blast of muscle-tissue pulling apart, one
sharp heartbeat like being whacked by a board,
white light, then an
   eternity of blackness?

Or would a heartburst be into
   greater being, pavilion of
dazzling crystal windows surrounding me,
each supporting column throbbing with
     greater resonance?

Or would it be in stages, first a
   clap of thunder, than a door in
     matter opening, then a long
runway among clouds, then a
   feeling of lighter-than-air, then
a sweeping perception of space itself,
     stretching way past China!

Heart catapult, canon of heart out of
   which the poor soul is shot!

Heart bellows for the paltry thoughts
of the brain! A

burst of ultra-Romantic music, the
   long rolling harmonies of
      Rachmaninoff, sliding
off the face of the earth wrapped in
      black velvet!

Heartburst panorama, stars across
emptiness, held together only by a

pulse, heart-pulse, steady and
   concentric, as our
own hearts might be seen from first
heartbeat to last, first pulse in the
   womb at the center of its ocean,
each pulse afterward a
   circle out to the edge, the
last beat wider than the
circumference of space itself, so when we

die we are at one with
God's dimension.

*(My heartbeat skips
at the very thought of it.)*

8/3

A BLUE LEAF

A blue leaf, triangle-shaped, black
    stemmed, where is the
tree it has drifted from?

A sharp gravel bit, black on one edge,
    white on the other, no
      bigger than a pearl, where is its
mother rock?

A raindrop, fallen among its brethren,
each one capable of reflecting the
    world, where is the
cascade of its source, where
    is its flood?

A road, traveled over and over by
    hunter, migration, adventurer,
      thief, where is the
original idea of *"road"* this
    road's branched off from?

These people, worried, coming and
going, coming and going, displaying
    faces of grief, joy,
intense blandness, where are the
first people, the stalwart, the
full-of-faith, the intrepid, these
    people descended from?

The soul, full of longing, restless,
  dissatisfied, trying on this
    way and that, shape-changing, almost

contented, almost
completely engulfed by light,

where is its perfect home, where

  is its resting place?

                                           8/5

HEAD WITHOUT IMAGES

Suddenly I want a head
   without images, without
sound, without sensations.

Give me an oval room carved from pure silver,
shiny and vast, with maybe
   only one round cloud in it,

a room like a surrounding circular
   observation window with
nothing to observe, total
   quiet, total silence,

a silence so huge the absence of
   sound makes a soft kind of
      whispering noise,

a place that's pictureless, the
   lovely endless tumult of
      movie snatches, floating
dialogue, complex situations imagistically
   portrayed

halted, its animation
suspended, hovering, as in the
instant before being projected. Since

imagery is our lives, and its
absence our deaths, let this

round dazzling space just
exist, surrounded by an equally
    transparent palpable

vastness,

a silence like a seed within silence, a

silveriness overlooking nowhere.

A sweetness.

8/7

BOY ON BICYCLE

A young boy just went by on a bicycle
  and he had the whole
universe inside him.

Head down, pumping the pedals, riding
  past my back garden fence,
glimpsed through the slats like those
  early rotating cinema wheels
where a still picture glimpsed between slits
    bursts into motion,
he had within his small determined
   blond head and
     energized body

the entire panorama of distant
stars and planets, the entire
mysterious shape of the universe, its
motions and projections, its
cycles and arcane procedures, the
coming to birth of galaxies, their
  inevitable snuffing out — red
    blaze, black aftermath —

and that pointed face with narrowed
  eyes as he passed
so energetically pedaling
and that lean intent body
had within them the
  godly cosmology that rules

each of our lives, prophets and
saints with their proclamations and
   sanctities, sciences of a
reality so fine only the highest
   mathematical language can
adequately represent them, a candle of
purest illumination burning at the
   far end of a green void, words whose
inspiration are on a level with the
   most glorious aurora borealis, shaking
its purple curtains above white ice,

all of history and all of time
imbedded in the consciousness of his
young blood and bones, even the key to his own
   enlightened evaporation
 before the Great Face of his Lord,

as he
pumped the two pedals with his sneakered
   feet past my garden fence

moving from one simple state of
   being to another, his pure

heart beating.

8/9

TWA FLIGHT TO ALBUQUERQUE

1

Crossing the sky above the clouds
there are many formations out the window
that look like mini-Hiroshimas
blazing with light.

2

Midflight in the journey of my life
I found myself in a bright sky…

3

Everyone thinks they're going somewhere.
The airplane seems headed in a direction.

Some may be thinking they're leaving somewhere.
We're actually just suspended in space.

The sum total at any one moment
of everything we've done, are, think and feel.

If we believe, we die believers.
If we doubt, we die doubters.

Somehow, cooped up in an airplane with

all these serious strangers, thinking, reading or sleeping,

this thought comes most vividly alive.

8/11

CLOUDS

Wavy clouds in blue New Mexico sky
(blue of turquoise necklace, huge blue eyes of
   otherworldly children
whose faces have evaporated into
thin air so only their suspended bright blue
       eyes remain),
one round fluffy cloud that looks like
it's named: *"Whatever-Happens-I'm-Happy,"*

one huge scimitar-shaped cloud as if
flung from west to east, that might be called:
"Cutting-Through-Untruth-to-Display-
   Pure-Endless-Space,"

one patch of disparate silvery-white paint daubs
from an original unity fleecily suspended,
that could be called: *"No-Piece-of-the-Puzzle-That-Doesn't*
   Contain-the-Whole,"

a great dark gray sky thunderhead covering
the entire eastern heavens, ominous, perhaps named
"So-Much-Noise-and-Flashing-Light
   in-This-Short-Life,"

bits of cloudy punctuation hanging above
   the purple western hills, pauses in the
      run-on sentence of sky exhaled in
one long breath from far behind vast visible space,

all these high cloudy signs of Allah's spacious elegant
manifestations, insubstantial bodies
lazily floating in the baby-blue pool of sky
    above sharp desert scrub and
        rugged gorge ravine,

as our hearts also rise from our
separately distinguished bodies

filled with these innermost

flashes of light.

                                                8/14

FALLING ASLEEP IN AN AIRPLANE ABOVE THE CLOUDS

We're making our way in a TWA airplane
    through the sky above
scattered fluffy clouds, puce, green and brown
    New Mexico topography glimpsed
between them down below, no
    habitations, lakes and snaky
       streams, and if I
should fall asleep up here, is it really
    sleeping? If the outward
sensual tentacles usually awake turn off and I
go inward to that unknown place where
sleep takes us, afloat, on fire, in
    freeze-frame or sailing through the
       sky *(ah, those allegedly erotic*
dreams of flying, flapping arms or just
cascading through the air)

can we call it sleep?

Sleep is the deer mother with her doe curled up
in her protective circle, paws and back legs
    surrounding it, on
pine needles on solid ground somewhere, hidden
    in a thicket,
but this is up in the air!

(Now the clouds outside the window are
    fragmentary cotton-puffs, each one

suspended with its cloud-shaped
    shadow underneath, just as I'm
sure underneath the plane a plane-shaped
    shadow crawls fuzzily
        along the ground.)
Would I close my eyes to open them in an
   even more spacious realm? What's to

keep us from sliding gently into eternity?
Flying elephants as light as cloud with
   spangled caparisons and outcurled
      trunks alongside us, or
Nefertiti's barge, cloud-bound, with her
   long-necked elegance and her
      retinue, up here among the
celestials, floating forward through sky.
Eyes wide open.

Just as mine are now, although I'm
   terribly sleepy. It's just that I
can't get used to my unconscious body in this
   metal cigarillo of an airplane
without being entirely awake. It's a
   contradiction. When you get this
high you want to keep watch, to see

God's Face in the clouds and sky, and
know it!

8/18

HEAD OF A PIN

This is a poem on the
   head of a pin, pushed
down into earth, maneuvered between
   grit and shale, puncturing
membranes between atoms, accompanied by the
   same music that accompanies the
deep birth of porpoises or the intrusion into a
   mountain of crackling glacier before the Mesozoic,
     a hissing between
       teeth of a bicycling postman on the
Isle of Ibiza making his rounds, only

this plummeting sound has a
   razor-like incisiveness, could
     slice through diamond, it's got the

acceleration of eagles' wings and the
determination of light traveling from the
beginning creational *ping*,

it actually goes down to the subatomic
level where desert dunes blow into
new shapes from one moment to the next,
where Mrs. Edgarton Plathborn is buried in her
ivory coffin to the sound of
   Tibetan trumpets on a
     high mountaintop in a
   purple sunset wrapped in blue silk,

but it keeps going, it wants to come out
not only on the other side of the world, but on
the other side of the universe, where a

bright yellow disk with the thickness of
eyelashes makes it way through space at
terrific speeds without leaving its
    place, a bafflement to
        all, and

light arrives in strings, taut as cello-wires,
along which faint golden sunbeams dance to an
intricate celestial tune.

My head makes a silhouette against
this distance, the

depth to which this poem aspires
is the same for gnats as for elephants,

soul-space nowhere in particular and
everywhere at once.

                                              8/20

THE DIVINE ORDER

If the whinny of horses were the cheep of
   birds instead, or if
     tiny sparrows made that
       sound horses make
that we made as kids by
   blowing through loose lips,

if boulders as big as houses were as
   light as feathers, and feathers were
heavy as lead, their aerial owners
     strong as gorillas,

if flowers barked at the moon all night
   from our back gardens, turning their
howling faces upward, and
   coyotes sang arias in
     contralto, deserts become
open air opera houses, although
snakes roared like lions and
tumbleweed nevermore tumbled, spreading their
   twigs like peacocks' tails
     to impress the more
       stationary brush —

but the way things are is the way things should be —

Divine Order shudders through
rifts in the earth's core,
shakes the rafters of the seas, collects

   clouds and
scatters seeds that by their
intricate seediness produce a
redwood here, an orchid
there, and none of them
      speaks *English!*

But they sing out themselves with the
glow of complete self-realization, rough bark for
    redwood, satin-smooth black orchid petals,
wide-eyed lemur, beady-eyed sloth
    upside-down in perfect comfort
        on his rainforest couch, asleep,
over alligator waters.

Each thing sings the song it sings,
light scattering down like the
coins tossed to songsters in
    subways to
reward their efforts.

Each core of us born in the
same crucible pearls and diamonds are
   born in, gleaming as if down at the
bottom of a shaft of darkness with a
beam of light that goes
straight to God's Throne, then
     sings the same
        chorus vegetables
sing in their cozy beds, but with
human timbre and voice, melodic leaps in

    deep space with the
        same nimble grace of
          gazelles, but with
only pure human agility, gazelle-leaps left to
      gazelles, while

the joyous shouts and anguished conundrums of humans are
fit to the human configuration, like
keys to their locks, to

open human doors to God's

every possible song.

                                                          8/23

I'D FORGOT UPON WAKING

I'd forgot upon waking
I'd won the celestial lottery allowed for
   those for whom gambling is prohibited,
small curved white feathers falling down in the air
     so slowly you could
   follow their fall onto the
silver tiles of the courtyard
     with your naked eye.

I'd forgot upon waking
that the giant rose-colored
   roc bird had transported me
to a foreign city with no known Gazetteer
  where people talk through jugs of water,
outline their eyes in blue sequins
     and discuss the cosmic distances between stars
more nonchalantly than the
  high price of
    trapezoids
at the Geometrical Market
    this morning.

I'd forgot upon waking
that the world had come to an end and
  started up again so quickly
nobody noticed, except trains going
    south went suddenly north,
  fish spoke fluent Japanese,
roadways were paved with edible

      nougat.

I'd forgotten all this in the intervening
hours of sleep, fragments
   sticking to my consciousness like
flecks of sand to legs of crabs as they
     sidle along a beach.

I'd forgotten you'd looked at me in a
certain way unusual even for you, and that
some little burden, as we kissed, had
flopped out of my heart and got
rinsed away in the kitchen sink with the
dishwater, releasing me that
one more crucial inch on my
    way to God.

But pigeon coo brought it all back
   soon enough,
and that I'd been made court fool at last
in the Cloud Palace, so long as I
   watched where my
glances landed, never looked either
king nor dignitaries
   straight in the face,

and kept
busy after sunrise.

                                              8/25

THE BOOK OF ROSES

1

I lay them at your feet.

If we zoom in
   we'll see their imperfections, worms
      among the petals, or if we

zoom in further, the jewel-like
   exquisite order of their atoms,
      the perfect *roseness* of each rose,

but if we leave them there as they are
with beads of water glistening in the
   light of Your Face,

then my offering may look less like
   broken heaps of straw, wretched
psychic knots, heart-
     beats gone syncopated to

sea-chant, water-flow, tide-rush
in and in past oily darkness
to a noble center, even
   deep black pitch —

redeemable.

2

They do not start up like
   pixies or
movie dwarves in rose costumes,

they do not untwine to become
   slithering serpents off to their
homes or to their
   semi-annual dinners.

These roses in their inert pile
do not resemble the matchwood reality
of so much of history's
   glamorized ideals
who've cost too much in human lives
to live up to their
promises —

they may not even live up to mine at my best —

they're spur of the moment, like
   this poem, their
imperfect scent is
   tangled up in the
smells of my own
decaying body at present, night-breath and
   night-sweat, with the

essences in this room at this hour, the
   basic scent, eagle

brooding over dark world, that
   smell, smell of
eagle, smell of dark world, utterly
      dusky smell of brooding —

although if I raise them up by just a little
above this world then their
own native pungency comes
rushing back to them,

pure rose essence
overpowering all the rest.

3

God gave us roses to tease us
by tokens of His Perfection
like petals thrown on a trail
   we can follow
      to find Him.

He's not behind appearances, He's
The Outwardly Manifest.

He's not within appearances, He's
The Inwardly Hidden,

these roses with their long stems like
one-legged stilts that
   got them here, trekking

     half the known world
to be piled on this doorstep,

these roses glittering here like
   hard arctic sunsets, a
     sudden blaze of
lightning white nimbus around each
   curve, each petal's
bent crescent,
  as dazzling as the
     constant rush of
   inaccessible Polynesian waterfalls,

calling out God's Names in all their
multifarious singularity, each
utterance and each
echo of that utterance

a perfect rose.

                                                 8/30

THE UNKNOWN QUANDARIES OF FATE

Nothing's come to me
  but a small boat
and on it some very small
  people, looking through a
magnifying glass at the
  small print on a contract in
which my mortality's at stake.

They nudge each other knowingly.
They share a private joke,
these almost indistinguishable
   Lilliputians who now know
more in detail about my
    fate than I do, also know

the waters the small boat
continues to navigate, rain or
shine, out past shadows to
either solid land like the
   islands and land masses
     Melville saw on his
early voyages, or else the open sea, weeks
or years in day-after-day
    sameness, vistas of

windy gray sky and heaving green waters,
occasional plop of dolphin or shark,
occasional watery upheaval of
   whale, and all while we're

navigating there's a self-enclosed
   world below where
ancient magnificent things go on
unbeknownst to those having to
live above water, unbeknownst to

myself whose entire
   enterprise this is, keeping my
meticulous logs, going from
day to day but watching them
   slip almost imperceptibly into
the grayness, having daily
   to battle inertia and

the unknown quandaries of fate.

                                                                    9/2

WHY ISN'T THE AIR FILLED WITH SINGING?

If it's the end of the world already
  how come angels aren't
passing out little conch shells of sweet tea
  and snow-frosted biscuits?

Why isn't the earth opening up
  right before our
  toes with great rifts going
all the way down to its molten core?

Why aren't black shapes of night passing
  before the moon?

Why isn't the air filled with
  singing?

THINGS PEOPLE LEAVE BEHIND

Think of all the things people never live to
    pick up, such as new prescription glasses,
deceased one day before they're ready, they
sit in a narrow cardboard box on a shelf
    the correct prescription for a pair of
        now-unseeing eyes.

Or a new tailored suit, pleats and inseams
    just so, length of sleeves to the
        perfect spot on the wrist,
the future wearer now wearing a winding sheet instead,
perfectly tailored to his body
set at its full length in the earth.

Or false teeth, toupees, hand-made
    shoes, prosthetic limbs,
their occupants now occupying an Elsewhere
where all these earthly accoutrements are
    utterly useless.

Now eyeglasses with wings on them
(for seeing into distant heavens),
suits of pure light illuminating companion
    spirits in flight,
teeth of fine-cut diamond for mouths
    sweet as new-mown grass where
words of utter simplicity and gratitude
pour out into surrounding
    streams of air and

symphonic harmonies —

a pair of tickets first class to the
    Bahamas, a
house on the hill just completed one
    day before its new owner's death,
mountains of things to which we are
    so attracted which make our
days livable,

left like Mexican pyramids in the
    encroaching rain forests of
time past, as we, in
perfectly functional
spirit bodies, with

all we now need
go on alone.

                                                                        9/6

WHEN FACING A DRAGON

When facing a dragon
keep your visor up, steam might
   fog your sight. Keep

your lower foot tightly wedged in a rock-crotch,
though not too tight for
instant egress. In other words,
be always ready to run, though
let no man know it.

Keep your sword arm flexible and
ahead of you, though you might
alternate raising and lowering
so the blood doesn't stagnate in one
   held position or other.

Keep, at all times,
your shield arm available to
quickly switch and defend, the
blast from dragon breath so far has been
unrecoverable, many a
scorched warrior just wasn't
   wary, looked always in
one spot, worried too much about
tail, claw or sharp scales to note
hurried breath and
   sudden sulfurous
     exhalation, for

be it known that dragons are Hell's
   forerunners, those gleaming
beautiful diamond sharp teeth glittery
     diversions from the
truth, so
don't let your guard down.

And for your eyes, this balm:
think continually of rose beds, lapping
green waters on shores, twinkling
   mountains, icecaps.

And for your heart as you
   strike and parry: have

your Beloved always at hand, her
sweet lips on your neck, her

face floating between you and
it, God-blessed and ignited

with supernatural
   grace, her long

arms along your sides, her
   nimble dance-feet. Let them

encompass yours. Become her
self entirely. Let her

sure light surround you, all dragons

take flight at that pure

transformation, at that implausible
    double sight, so

stalwart yet as
lithe as candle flame, wind-bending,

sweet as true faith is

on any
dark mountainside.

                                                                         9/11

ANOTHER LIFE

As I sat on the john reading a New Yorker
a most crystalline little flying thing landed on the
top of the page I was reading, and
   since I'm so nearsighted and was
     reading without glasses, I could
inspect this insect with nonchalant impunity, and
   see its trim almost athletic and
     youthful vigor. It

stood on the page for a moment, thin little legs
   braced, angled slightly so its
front end was higher than its back, though
   maybe that's just the way it's built,
it waved its antennae around a little, or
  flexed them from side to side, not like a
   horse shaking its mane but like someone
newly arrived somewhere getting the lay of the land.

It washed them for a moment, front legs as
   scrubbers, and I
imagined this ubiquitous insect process like
   windshield wipers to effect
     clearer vision.

That done, it stood again, perhaps lost in
   thought, then started up its
exploratory stroll. Up to the

top of the page, along the top edge for a moment,

     those hair-thin
   legs straddling it, then along the
level top of the pages that
    remained to be read, then

suddenly down in, and I panicked slightly that it'd
get lost and inadvertently squashed, that I might
forget it's there and close the
magazine, for though it looked in perfect
   health and vigor, by the
world's standards it was frail, no
bigger than a nail paring, extremely
   skeletal. So I

tilted the magazine and caught
sight of it between the pages from behind,
saw its oval rump with those
bandy bow legs of it trotting along,
  down and down it went. I

fanned the pages in hopes of finding it to
   let it fly free *(I had also*
wondered at its constant options: to fly or to walk.
It'd landed flying out of the air on this
magazine, which was a stationary
   object in its world. But what did it
mean to him, a source of food? A new

vacation spot on its travels? Large
   white beaches and occasional cartoons?
And then it could walk or fly as it

*chose. I
marveled at the ingenuity of the
creature with this
constant set of possibilities, one as
  wonderful as just taking off to*

*somewhere else, an enviable
  situation, possible to humans only if
one's rich and flamboyant enough to go*

*off to an airport on a
whim and buy a ticket to, say,
Biarritz).*

So I followed it along with my nearsighted
eyes, this tiny gnat-like looking job with its
glittery transparent wings, and from

behind, so squat and bandy-legged,
  it looked like some
beer-bellied slouch at a ball game waddling between
    bleachers, then it

disappeared! I
looked for it through the
    pages, but

poof!

Gone!

So I returned to my reading, read a
page, turned it,
    and *lo!*

There it was!

Then,
without further notice

it lifted itself into the

air, those two glittery
wings

soundlessly whirring, and

flew away!

                                            9/12

THE NEW YORK PHILHARMONIC ON TV PLAYING BRAHMS' FIRST SYMPHONY

Kurt Mazur becomes Brahms.
I love the way he sometimes makes a little
   cupping gesture close to his
     chest with his right hand *(no baton)*
then a sweeping arc with his left.

One violinist is a secret composer of
   microtonal chamber music his wife will
find in a trunk after his death and he will become
posthumously world famous.

Another violinist wanted to be a banker, and
assiduously follows the stock market,
    visible on his shiny bald head.

The woman flautist is married to an
   eminent veterinarian who treats exotic
pets and writes books. Their daughter is
     dyslexic.

The French horn player with the ponytail
is surprisingly good at training horses,
   which he does at his
     Upper State New York farm on weekends
when he is not playing
   Wagner or Mahler or Brahms
     with the orchestra.

The page-boy lady bassoonist is a
    sexual torch.

Kurt Mazur's face is a taut mirror into which
all Brahms' music flows as he
    faces the orchestra.
The notes of the music seem to be combing the
   few wispy white hairs on his head.

One of the cellists will be dead by this
    time next year, and the
  last thing he hears will be
a stray melodic strain from this symphony,
with its victorious angelic breathing.

Ah, the French horn section now, mostly
serious bearded military-looking
   dudes, blows a
wave of ecstatic mellowness, now the

trombonists, two in their sixties, white-haired,
business-like, the

Fourth Movement swells, then

that familiar opening theme from the 1940's
radio program, *(was it The Voice of Firestone?)*
Doesn't matter. Ladies playing flutes, having
   had their hair done just this
afternoon for tonight's performance, elegant in
    black tulle.

Now a camera shot over a violin past the
    music on the music stand to a
fuzzily out-of-focus Kurt Mazur in the
      background,
pan of the violinists, some with
eyes closed really feeling the music,
fingers on strings and bows back and forth
    across them, making all this
      miraculous sound!

It all comes together in an
oceanic crescendo, and we see
tuxedo'd Kurt doing a
    vibrating little dance
  on the podium, and with
no score in front of him, it all
    just there inside him, as if the
whole symphony were a
familiar European city, say, in
Austria, where he knows
all the streets by heart, all the side
boulevards with scrumptious pastry shops, all the
    great outdoor cafés,
special restaurants for full-course meals,
knows where the city's giant
     river flows —
little out-of-the-way parks,
the best places for skyline viewing —
to watch thunder clouds gather over the hills.

A short haircut Chinese cellist

leans forward with his cello.

The French horn player with the moustache
takes a deep breath.

A solemn but pretty
blond violinist's fingers tremble.

9/17

INVENTORY

1

The blue patch across the forehead, the
   idle ivory handle on the saddle,
elephantine gargantuans, one on each side,
   a waste of time in green foil,
scars where most have slurs, slurs
   on top of scars going upstairs,
sailors in long lines, ships at sea, the
   sea in a long line, unlike its
usual helter-skelter choppiness,
the red eyeglass, the skin-splint, the
   skinflint, Sinn Féin on a good day,
there is no open space, loud enough
   or clear,
over the hill, overlooking the rill, a
   gale in full sail.

All is well.

2

A scar on the forehead just under the
   hairline, from a
     disremembered blow,
piles of glossy black and white photos of the
   perfect body, malformed by
     practice,

a lifeless side and a lively side,
a rose tree and a fig tree,
a blue sky and a deep hole,
sand bars that cross the horizon and
   disappear in a sea of blowing reeds,
elephant bones in a sun-dappled
     clearing, no other wildlife
       in sight,

Scandinavian bread in an outdoor café
   with strong coffee,
a slow Gypsy song passionately sung
   by a geranium wall,
elegant gestures by unknown people who
   make them then fade away,
solemn pronouncements made by people who
   make them then fall apart,

an old egg and a new shoe,
a long pipe and a short attention span,
a broken tooth and a good eye for detail,
a sound unlike any sound heard before
   as of grief unappeased or joy unexpected,

a flinging of thought beyond its usual perspective,
a flight of fancy that in fact is
   based on fact,
a perfect roundness and an imperfect whole,
a saintliness that precedes and follows us
wherever we go.

But I stand on ceremony.
The country is moving away, leaving its
   citizens unmoored.
A smug indifference infects the passersby
at the delicate corpse
   whose features are almost
     Egyptian.

There is so little time to say hello or bid
   farewell
except if you become the paper it's
   written on, or the
ink it's written in,
and the wind turns you like a weather vane.

But the air is still.

The wind too has gone home.

I shall teach the black birds to say
   boo!

9/25

A PLACE NOT UNLIKE PITTSBURGH

Although I've never been to Pittsburgh, but
   I like the title, it has a
smart click to it, in spite of the fact that

where I wanted to go in this poem
was much more tropical than Pittsburgh, actually
rain forest-like, tangly with
   creepers and low-hanging vines

across our blanched faces of fear and anticipation.

A place not unlike
Eden, in fact, where animals of prodigious as well as
microscopic size pass and mingle, some of the
smaller ones getting free rides, sometimes even
free dinners, from the bigger ones,
horny-headed ones with scarlet and mauve
   stripes and gold ears,
blushing tousle-haired ones with black faces and
   yellow zigzags, topped off with
small pronged horns, their hair
   woolly, their eyes
     soulful.

Lakes as wide as thought.

Trees so dense with shadow they look
   sunken. It's all

forest, ferns, intricate pathways naturally trod,
and at dead center, a place one could say is

not totally unlike Pittsburgh, but is actually
lodges laid out like
   spokes of a wheel, so that the

Chieftainess, who goes around in stringy
   garments and daubs her
      face with red berries,

can sing her holy songs at the
center, her

revelatory songs about the
whimsical behavior of the skies and the unending
mercy of an Unseen and Magnificent
God.

                                                             9/27

GUNSHOT OR BACKFIRE

Gunshot or backfire, backgrounded by a
   siren, 2 a.m. in the
morning. The Lord has released
some energy going either
one way or another, a blue bottle on a
   doorstep filled with smoke
or a boiled egg falling in slow-motion down the
   front of a forty story office building on an
empty street.

A face full of life becomes frozen as a
   face full of anguish, hardly a
fitting punctuation to a
childhood on bicycles and an
    adolescence as a shy
      astronomer.

Pink biscuits float on a dark stream.

A life like a clenched fist on a
linoleum tabletop suddenly

changed into a swan opening its
too large wings in a too-small
space unable to lift off and
 fly away. Its black eye-mask
   flashes. Its feathery
white breast heaves.
It has to demolish the room it's in, it

    has to expand past these
four small walls on earth where the

heart dwells too long confined in its
vicious circle of knotty feelings and
rotational thoughts.

Swans float overhead on their
way to the equator. Ocean of sky

in which we are drowned.

Down here among subaqueous vegetation.

Live face suddenly made into mask of shock by a
single gunshot, a life
   exploded from its confinement,

freed past its usual perimeters, diametrically
    opposed to the salt grain, the
       pink eraser, the
dollar bill. This

poignant death, like a

flea pressed between thumbnails,

free of chromium and gears, left

among green leaves and pure waters,

free-flying singer of celestial songs
gliding without arms past
    silhouettes of pain

into a bakery of pure glory
with its strong smells of new bread.

                                              9/28

ON A SHOESTRING

Spray the buzzard white and
    watch the swan.
The hoot owl sounds like a twelve-piece
    jazz band in New Orleans on a
        late Tuesday night after
            ribs in October.
Three small paper boats are seen through
one squinting eye as the Spanish Armada
ignites the horizon with war and certain death.
Sand castles become high rise real estate
oceanfront property worth millions.
Small angels proliferate in the miniature
woods that runs behind the town.
They filter down between pine needles and
    spruce twigs, they
  ride foreheads of deer
      between incipient antlers.

They herald the arrival of air and sunshine
like ancient trumpeters of Timbuktu.
They echo across the gulf.
The gulf between these elegant or inelegant
    fabrications and the
firmly outlined hard-edged so-called reality all around me
  as I sit in my green flannel
pajamas on the side of my

bed writing this.

10/1

NAME OF GOD

1

The Name of God came haunting down the hall
and dazzled all our eyes and ears and
   hearts, and made us

swoon into this hard physical life,
and we'll be wakened and called back

and then we'll leave this world as
things departing from shadows
leave their shadows in heaps like
   old clothes at the
      door

through which we'll all depart to go back to that
chanting school, those corridors of
   pure reverberation through

pine woods, mountain cloud, egrets hovering in an
   updraft, sunlight on
     rock, sun twinkle on

stream gush, that exquisite

Name of God again, repeated by God's own
speech on the tongue of everything.

The Name of God foghorns

out at sea where
blackened darkness deepens within darkness.

The Name of God suspended in amoebas hovering just below
   the surface tension of a moonlit lake.

The Name of God in the first movements of an eaglet inside its
high shell on a cliff beaten by
   wind, its brother and sister eaglets
     starting to stretch inside
their shells at exactly the
       same time.
The Name of God in the high wind beating against them.

The Name of God in rigging out at sea
   the high wind beats against.
The Name of God in the audible beats that
   accompany the wind, in the
silent beats as well as the
ones sounded out, the lapping as well as the
   silence as the sea recedes.

Laughter followed by the silence of death.

The Name of God in them both.

2

And who hears the Divine Name being
   recited over and over with each

    pump of our blood through the
Tunnels of Love of our veins? Each

drip of ice water off a glacier into a
    pool so translucently clear
the entire sky of the world is reflected
with all its gnats and all its
    migrating birds? Who

hears on the tip of its tongue the Name of God being
    told? The first shift of
glance of a newborn, and
    no sharp sound was made?

The doctor leaning in with his
    stethoscope is the Divine Name's
heavenly P.A. system into his

own ears from every pulse he hears?

The billionaire leaning closer in to his
    telephone receiver in penthouse
        solarium as the deal is
clinched, who hears the Name of God so clearly
    spoken, but may
        mistake it for a sum?

The baseball outfielder who hears it as the
    ball zooms by, or the *thunk* of it
        into his mitt?

The chipmunk who hears it as an acorn
   falls from highest oak
      branches into his paws?

The mud slide in Venezuela heard by the
shocked villagers below?

The butterfly's flight pattern as God's Name on a
breeze shifts ever-so-slightly to the
      east?

Entire populations as they scurry to their jobs?

Entire populations of underwater denizens
as the natural booms and creakings in the
   deep
     resound in their bones?

A single diamond miner as his axe slips
    uncovering a gleam?

An ancient derelict who positions her head on her
pile of rags and slips into dream?

She hears it. It

reaches to the bottom of her toes.
It leaves no stone unturned.

Audible by all,
it takes no prisoners. It's

audible now, cricket in the

silent center of night, cricket out

in the night

under a

starless sky.

10/7

THE SOUL

The body, God bless it, many, many times
   weaker than the soul,

falls aside at the moment of death
with the sound of falling autumn leaves,
dry crinkling of old mummies,
the sound of shovelfuls of dirt being
    delivered down a hole,
the sound of air moving through air, it's
   that insubstantial, but Oh

how brave it was in its heyday, stood out
    on an airplane's wing,
scaled oblique rock faces hand over heartbeating
   hand and lived *(for a time)* to
tell the tale, married and engendered
  more of itself, little human
     caterpillars alternately
       fleshy and furry, in clothes,
   dancing at parties, or

out of clothes settling down naked into
    Niagara Jacuzzis engulfed in
      steam.

How robust the body was until chicken pox or
   paper cut showed it its
     vulnerability, none so

great as actually being ripped aside like an
old glove to be ceremoniously or
   uncemoniously discarded at the

moment of death for the exit of the beloved
soul, the infinitely stronger of the two,
to carry on, catapult up and
   out, roller coaster
up and up with, this time,

the sound of the formation of soap bubbles
   on a gossamer ledge,

the siphoning sound of hummingbirds
   drinking hibiscus nectar, the

making of a spider web in a shaft of sunlight,

silent yawn of a white tiger in Siberian hills,

the sound of multitudes of
   feathers
     accelerating in
heady atmospheres, the

song of a single bamboo flute from a
   single Peruvian herdsman at
dusk with his placid herd,

stronger than a redwood grove, stronger than
the seven seas combined,

stronger even than the seven heavens
    opening up to receive it —

the soul.

Singing.

10/9

NEW PHYSICS

"*First of all, time originates from a
   central point and spreads out to its
edges like a circle,*" he said,
pushing his spectacles back up to in front of
   those topaz eyes!

"*It's space that's consecutive, and chronological,
   spatialogical, time just expands to
     everywhere evenly,*" his old voice
filling the corner of the universe we were in
   and flowing past its edges.

"*Perceptions are angels falling and rising
   freely through space, giving apparent
form to what is essentially nothingness,
making us think we see
such things as rock faces, canyons, rogue
   rivers, earthquakes, wars, famine,
infanticide, suicide...*" He made his
mouth a grim line to show the
difficulty in such concepts. Then he

smiled a smile of diamond gleams against
   green velvet.
"*Laughter is actually the clapping of faraway hands,
weeping the heart of a large celestial
   beast tenderly washing out a few
things, obtruding into
   this world by the intensity of its*

  rubbing." His face
was like the earth with clouds passing across it,
darkening then lightening again, alternatingly
  cool and hot.

*"Our lives fold back into themselves constantly
like a constantly evolving origami figure
in the hands of a beneficent giant in a
  place that is opposite to
    total darkness."* He winked at me

and we slid in slow motion down an
avalanche of household furniture and
  the latest fashions from
    cave dwellers to the
      present day.

"We're helpless to resist," he sang, like
  glass swans on a placid lake
    all taking melodious
flight at the
  same time into
different skies.

"Nothing is as it seems," he continued, *"but
  our hearts are like a
beam of light moving
    forward through a tunnel at
velocities the envy of distant
    galaxies."* Actual

star-twinkle appeared in his hair at
this remark, his hair elongated like the
    mist of the Milky Way.

"I have so much more to say," he said, the
sound of his voice trailing off like the
    afterimage of silver.

"I have nothing more to say," it echoed,
    back and forth like the
tail of a toy dog.

Like the tail of a real
  full grown dog that
    barks once then

runs off down a
  green hill.

10/12

GUEST SPEAKER

Death is eloquent beyond eloquence:
   guest speaker at a banquet
where all the food turns to stone.

Flight of birds through an icy sky that becomes
   a block of ice like
birds trapped in amber.

Word turned to ash on the tongue.

Sight turned to utter stillness. The
last picture on the retina a Polaroid for all eternity.

Flexible blissful face in full sunlight.
Look of horror frozen against a
   full moon.

Death raises a glass to a toast in which
all the participants assess their present state,
the map of trails and rest stops along the way
that led them here, ice swan melting
   backwards, light shimmering which is

actual darkness giving way to formlessness.

Death smiles and the
windows brim with light.

Death furrows an impenetrable brow

and darkness becomes a dusk rose pinned
on a blue shirt.

There's no one left in the hall now
but death, glass still raised.

The music begins.

10/13

TOTALLY UNIQUE

Behind this stone is another stone,
shaped identically, and behind that stone
is an infinity of stones arching back and
   back, a suspension bridge of
identical shadow stones entering thought
   realms and existence realms inhabited by

a single lit candle, a multitude of
dwarf angels, a stand of ponderosa pine trees
   of celestial texture, and behind
the lit candle, dwarf angels and ponderosa
pine trees are suspension bridges of
identical presences going back and
   back into realms unknown and
     previously unexplored,

and behind these words scratched out in my
notebook after dawn
lie suspension bridges of identically
   shaped and meaning-charged
locutions, but in
   each realm back in which they
     lie the meanings
change and deepen, one might mean

a herd of stampeding unicorns down an
apricot-colored hill, another might mean
the spectral brooms of ancient
German grandmothers as preserved in

fable, while another, way back in a

realm of constantly strumming zither music
(also vibrating back and back, each
  note echoing in realms further
    removed) one of these
words might sit on a tall silver
   pedestal in blinding incandescent
     resplendence with a
    jagged crown of gold light flashing
     all around it,
its pronunciation sounding out above the
    strummed chords and
ascending twinkling notes,

so that all things, tables, shadows,
door knobs, nose hairs, thoughts so
deep sound daren't plummet their
   depths, have
real reverberations in spaces we may
know nothing whatever about, and

even our selves, our very elusive
on-again, off-again selves with their
phantom outlines and consistent
   habits and obsessions, to say
    nothing of their delicate shadings of
feeling and sensitivity to a good
   story or an insoluble
    tragic situation,

these selves also have behind them,
shaped identically but inhabiting
other spaces, other rooms,
linked infinitely back and back into
    realm after realm,
selves in looping suspension bridges of selfhood back
to a final starting point, a
   silver mist on the tip of a
     needle held up in
the first space of creation, God's

Light having imbued each self with an
initial serious resonance,
garlanded like a
prize racehorse
with all the resplendent
  words it will use in its
lifetime, all the chairs it will
    sit in, all the smiles
exchanged with other selves, all the
handshakes and copulations,

the deserts of the skies populated with
mirror images going off in all
   directions, this

stone sitting by the side of the
road only the latest
messenger, the latest message from all its

spatial relatives of just how

such a stone should look, just how
such a stone should sit in

just that sunlight casting

just that shadow.

10/14

POST TRAUMATIC STRESS

How did Roman soldiers do when they
   came back from a war — say, the
Punic Wars — did they
slip right back into society, farm their
  acres, make clay pots, sell
    wares in the marketplace,
perfectly natural?

Or did they stomp around in spite, resentful,
maladjusted, angry at everybody, did they

go off their nut every time something, even something
trivial like a door slamming, grind of
chariot axle or shout in the distance,
reminded them of the stench of battle, the
nightmarish yells and screams, thrusting a
sword into a body and wrenching it out again
to the sound of anguished sighing, the

sight of dark blood oozing into the
   ground from around
     bashed-in armor, the vision of broken faces,
slashed arms and legs, piles of bodies, clouds of steam and
     death hovering over black
   battlefields,

did these young men just set their
jaws and stare straight ahead with their eyes and hearts
and go about their business?

Or did they sob in the night when
no one was looking, out of earshot,

did they get down on their
knees and bawl like babies
in the remote cities and villages
of the Roman Empire,

feeling the pain of human helplessness
and the irrevocable

rape of their souls?

                                                                             10/16

LOST AND FOUND

There is a hand
lying at rest on a sunset windowsill
holding a small white camellia
to the sound of slow mandolin strumming
as its owner muses on the
   perfection of her day
      and the perfection of God.

Does it belong to anyone?

There is a golden stallion
on a silhouette horizon against
   deepening blue sky,
it tosses its mane and sparks fly,
it beats its hooves and gallops off down the
   hill to run across
      wide valleys until it
reaches foaming sea.

Did anyone lose it, the
wild stallion of their
   innermost heart?
Can anyone claim it as their own?

There is a self
so self-contained, so empty of
self, the entire Milky Way of
constellations and planetary motions fits
  into it with room to spare,

it moves and is motionless, it
    acts and relinquishes action
with the same simple grace, it's a
self that has let go of itself to let
God govern it and give it life.

Does anyone long for this
  state, this
    hallowed goal?

There's a small mouse
who lives in the wall
and runs back and forth behind the
wainscoting, tiny tap of tiny
    paws as it
scurries along. It contains the

universe as well, it looks out its
eyes with the same
pure confidence in
God's bounty, it has its

sweet moments and its
moments of terror.

Has anyone heard the mouse's call?

Has anyone heard the mouse's call?

KICK A BLUE BALL

Lick the salt wound, laugh the
   licorice ice pole, dance to the
jig of liquidation blues, see the

top of it all blow to smithereens in a
globule of smoke, see the

old guy on the green horse lie
   down on the track and die.

It's a rush blur, a bluish rose, a
   blank screen, it's a

blue shield, a blink and then it's
gone, a severe
   snowstorm so
serene it's like a bank heist done in
   slow motion, covering
everything in dry
     ice.

Race to the finish, sing for your
   supper, dine with the
queen on a molecule spur,

listen wholeheartedly to the
   brass band play inside your
inner ear as hope begins to
play chess with despair and

win on a cold windy beach in a
gray day in Paradise — the

whole thing beginning to grow
dimmer as the glow grows low

and encompasses us all.

All, all.

Kick a blue ball.

10/22

THEFT IN A FOREIGN COUNTRY

1

I woke up suddenly from sleep
   sitting up on the wooden
bus station bench to find someone had
stolen my wallet from my jacket
pocket, my luggage which was
sitting at my feet, and my watch.
What else? There wasn't anything
   else for them to steal. My glasses, which
they kindly left on my face. *Thanks.*

I looked around the nearly empty station I'd
staggered into only a couple hours before
at the three or four bedraggled travelers,
   also snoring,
at the dark night outside the arch,
the sound of escaping steam from a
   locomotive down the tracks.

I got up, totally helpless, totally
   stripped, feeling totally
naked and totally lost, black
   liquid swirling at the
      base of my brain, my
heartbeat voodoo tattoo terrible to
   hear, I could kill, scream, no one to
kill, no one to scream to, wake up these
fellow passengers, maybe they've been

stripped of everything too, let them have a
   little more blissful time of
      ignorance if they have, I

stumbled out of the station and out into
alien night, now not so
   soft and friendly as it had been when I'd
stumbled into the station exhausted, now not so
close to me like a sweet lover, now a
furious and evil night lurking in its own
   shadows, waiting to
pounce on me, a passing
   porter, possibly the

bastard who
took all my stuff, I thought of
   trying to ask him or
     tell him what
happened, but realized it'd be
useless to try to translate
everything so he'd
 get the point, plus I was now
furious as well as tired, and
  scared and frustrated and
disappointed in these people, the
   whole trip, this
hard-hearted country full of thieves…

I walked on into the night thinking really
black thoughts, hands jammed deep into
the pockets of my only possession

which possessed me, giraffe legs fitted so
neatly into my pants legs, oriole breath, a
    whistle under my breath, owlets in the
eaves of my eye sockets, I could hear all those

wild windy spaces in my head, as if my
head were a way-station between two
thunder cloud eternities. I made

fists like two burning planets just
born from some
galactic collision, voices as of
    slithering things, maybe
worms, maybe footless reptiles going in
all directions through grass, called

my name, I saw through the
tunnel of the closing-in darkness to the
blue backlit river just in front of me where
splendid women were washing
    clothes on rocks, only they had

long wings which hung down from their backs, and
the live ends like cat's tails curled around
them slightly as they worked, and there was a

moon like an eye had burned through the
blanket of darkness to my
ghostly soul and was peering
intently down into me, and I

fell on my knees when a green light-filled
figure appeared of an old
fern-headed man laughing and holding his
hands in prayer position in front of him, and I

suddenly remembered God with a
   force that could have
      exploded a building, a desert

wind full of slamming doors blew across me,
I clutched my sides and saw the

corridors of my mortality flood with
light, a light blinding enough but also
palpably soothing, a black river of

light like a mother's touch, like the
brushing of lips against ear a
lover might do, I was

way out in space in one of God's galaxies, on
earth, where a
hooting train had delivered me.

2

Into a blue sky
darts a red bird.

Into a green sea

dives a white fish.

Into a black night
jumps a yellow flame.

Into a wild heart
falls a ray of peace.

10/25

NOT FOR SALE

As he came into the town he
   noticed boxes and boxes of
long-stemmed and short-stemmed roses, all
    colors, red, violet, orange, snow-white,
vendors on sidewalks, vendors from
horse-drawn carts, vendors in vans — piles and
   piles of roses, and he thought,
"Ah, what a romantic race, a
   people at last for whom
beauty is a mode of communication, and
    on such a grand scale!"

He didn't know, poor man, that it was
   because of the Rose Beast, who
comes into town at dusk and has to have
hundreds and hundreds of roses to eat in order
to *not* eat their tenderest children,
a monster who
   thrives on beauty but eats it
    savagely, who depends on the
mystical form of the rose, but only
to fill his stomach.

To see him
grab bunches of
gorgeous rainbow roses and push them,
   bud first, into his
gaping jaws, is
   indescribably horrific. And

more horrific still are the looks on the vendors' faces
    as they're
forced to gaze into that slobbering maw until
      he's eaten his fill.

As the man slowed his car and pulled to the
side of the road and got out to buy a
bunch of long-stemmed roses that had
caught his eye, and walked up to the
vendor with a bill in his hand, he
realized something strange was afoot. Because

the vendor looked up at him with a

long mournful gaze, a rose-shaped

tear in each eye, and said:

"Sorry…
Not for sale."

THE BEAUTY FEAST

If I draw the little figure of a garden on a
   toothpick, for in this world it seems
these things are ignored,
or if I etch a leafy landscape with my
   fingernail on a frosty glass,
or see the tops of trees towering skyward
   in the flat mirror of a rain puddle,
or if I see flower and leaf forms
   in your eyes and wish to
keep them there long enough to
   stroll through, under a
sunlit trellis, across grass, down a
   dark trail between oaks, the
sparkling sound of a river swollen after rain,

if I engrave it on the antler of a
   young buck bounding off,
in the corner of a letter bound for Singapore,
   the terraces and hidden pools, if I
draw it in invisible ink on the
   inside of a spool of thread in some
Third World industrial factory knitting socks,
or on the backs of shirt-collars being shipped to
Africa or Spain, just a

tiny drawing, or on a blank page in a
   library book before it's
dropped through the return slot,
or on the stub of a stadium ticket, on the

    shaft of an umbrella, those banks of
rose trees, hedges making
      labyrinths, splashing fountains,

if I just sketch it quickly on a
snow bank, a sick child's eyelid, a
wren's beak, a worm's accordion cummerbund,

or perhaps just say it, don't
      etch it at all, just
repeat this poem to the migrating
butterfly, its wing-pattern packed in its
DNA ready for flight,
to a grasshopper before it leaps in the
  night to its vibrating lover nearby,
to a distant galaxy exploded into being a
      billion years ago but
  just now
    · becoming visible to our eyes,

or perhaps, if that's too much, I
keep it to myself, walk among
    clank of train yards, the
clashing shrill rhythm of factories, the rush of
newspaper printing presses producing the
  Sunday Edition,
    aerodynamics labs with their
thunderous whirr of supersonic jets being
      tested,

if I stand near the loud *whoosh* of

    New York traffic and just
think it, or near the
giant crashing
    breakers off Cornwall,
breaking-up Antarctic ice floes, boiling
    volcanic rifts rumbling in
Borneo, Japanese
   car factories running full tilt,
Mongolian electric plants, if I just

silently imagine the meandering topaz stream that
flows through it, through the heart's garden, on its
   way into heaven, through every
living person, man, woman and child,
    the foliage of richness in
      each of us, if I just

hold it in my own heart in all its microscopically
perfect detail, the
buzz of gnat the only sound audible,
play of late afternoon light through leaves
   the only sight visible,
odors of living greenery and foliage the only aroma
    traceable

to its Original Source...

                                              10/28

INDEX OF TITLES

A Blue Leaf   64
A Place Not Unlike Pittsburgh   106
A State of Love   55
A Very Small White Horse   58
Another Life   95
Boy on Bicycle   68
Clouds   72
Correspondences   12
Dappled Place   25
Falling Asleep in an Airplane above the Clouds   74
Flower Shapes   10
Forgiveness   28
Funeral   30
Goldfish   17
Guest Speaker   123
Gunshot or Backfire   108
Half-Circle of Light   19
Happiness   42
He Wrote on the Walls   39
Head Without Images   66
Head of a Pin   76
Heartbeat of the Skies   21
Heartburst   62
Inventory   103
I'd Forgot upon Waking   81
Kick a Blue Ball   133
Lost and Found   131
Musical Instrument   45

Name of God   112
New Physics   120
Not For Sale   140
On a Shoestring   111
Ordering Chinese   23
Picture of the Garden   9
Placement   50
Post Traumatic Stress   129
Spinning Top   32
Story of the Woman Whose Head was a Rosebush   34
Symphony   99
TWA Flight to Albuquerque   70
The Beauty Feast   142
The Book of Roses   83
The Divine Order   78
The Ecstatic Drinker   48
The New York Philharmonic on TV Playing Brahms' First
The Soul   117
The Story of the Blind Landscape Architect   52
The Story of the Czechoslovakian Button-Maker   14
The Unknown Quandaries of Fate   87
Theft in a Foreign Country   135
Things People Leave Behind   90
Totally Unique   125
When Facing a Dragon   92
Why Isn't the Air Filled with Singing?   89
Winding Green Tendril   36

ABOUT THE AUTHOR

Born in 1940 in Oakland, California, Daniel Abdal-Hayy Moore's first book of poems, *Dawn Visions*, was published by Lawrence Ferlinghetti of City Lights Books, San Francisco, in 1964, and the second in 1972, *Burnt Heart/Ode to the War Dead*. He created and directed *The Floating Lotus Magic Opera Company* in Berkeley, California in the late 60s, and presented two major productions, *The Walls Are Running Blood*, and *Bliss Apocalypse*. He became a Sufi Muslim in 1970, performed the Hajj in 1972, and lived and traveled throughout Morocco, Spain, Algeria and Nigeria, landing in California and publishing *The Desert is the Only Way Out*, and *Chronicles of Akhira* in the early 80s (Zilzal Press). Residing in Philadelphia since 1990, in 1996 he published *The Ramadan Sonnets* (Jusoor/City Lights), and in 2002, *The Blind Beekeeper* (Jusoor/Syracuse University Press). He has been the major editor for a number of works, including *The Burdah* of Shaykh Busiri, *The Prayer of the Oppressed*, by Imam Nasir al-Dar'i, both translated by Shaykh Hamza Yusuf, and the poetry of Palestinian poet, Mahmoud Darwish, translated by Munir Akash. He is also widely published on the worldwide web: *The American Muslim, DeenPort*, and his own website and poetry blog, among others: *www.danielmoorepoetry.com*, and *www.ecstaticxchange.wordpress.com*. He served as poetry editor for *Islamica Magazine*, and *Seasons Journal*, and a new translation by Munir Akash of *State of Siege*, by Mahmoud Darwish, from Syracuse University Press in 2010. The Ecstatic Exchange Series is bringing out the extensive body of his works of poetry (a complete list of published works on page 2).

POETIC WORKS by Daniel Abdal-Hayy Moore
Published and Unpublished

Dawn Visions (published by City Lights, 1964)
Burnt Heart/Ode to the War Dead (published by City Lights, 1972)
This Body of Black Light Gone Through the Diamond (printed by Fred Stone, Cambridge, Mass, 1965)
On The Streets at Night Alone (1965?)
All Hail the Surgical Lamp (1967)
States of Amazement (1970)

Abdallah Jones and the Disappearing-Dust Caper (published by The Ecstatic Exchange/Crescent Series, 2006)
'Ala ud-Deen and the Magic Lamp
The Chronicles of Akhira (1981) (published by Zilzal Press with Typoglyphs by Karl Kempton, 1986) (published in Sparrow on the Prophet's Tomb, The Ecstatic Exchange, 2010)
Mouloud (1984) (A Zilzal Press chapbook, 1995) (published in Sparrow on the Prophet's Tomb, The Ecstatic Exchange, 2010)
Man is the Crown of Creation (1984)
The Look of the Lion (The Parabolas of Sight) (1984)
The Desert is the Only Way Out (completed 4/21/84) (Zilzal Press chapbook, 1985)
Atomic Dance (1984) (am here books, 1988)
Outlandish Tales (1984)
Awake as Never Before (12/26/84) (Zilzal Press chapbook, 1993)
Glorious Intervals (1/1/85) (Zilzal Press chapbook, ?)
Long Days on Earth/Book I (1/28 – 8/30/85)
Long Days on Earth/Book II (Hayy Ibn Yaqzan)
Long Days on Earth/Book III (1/22/86)
Long Days on Earth/Book IV (1986)
The Ramadan Sonnets (Long Days on Earth/Book V) (5/9 – 6/11/86) (published by Jusoor/City Lights Books, 1996) (republished as Ramadan Sonnets by The Ecstatic Exchange, 2005)
Long Days on Earth/Book VI (6-8/30/86)
Holograms (9/4/86 – 3/26/87)
History of the World (The Epic of Man's Survival) (4/7 – 6/18/87)
Exploratory Odes (6/25 – 10/18/87)

The Man at the End of the World (11/11 – 12/10/87)
The Perfect Orchestra (3/30 – 7/25/88) (published by The Ecstatic Exchange, 2009)
Fed from Underground Springs (7/30 – 11/23/88)
Ideas of the Heart (11/27/88 – 5/5/89)
New Poems (scattered poems, out of series, from 3/24 – 8/9/89)
Facing Mecca (5/16 – 11/11/89)
A Maddening Disregard for the Passage of Time (11/17/89 – 5/20/90) (published by The Ecstatic Exchange, 2009)
The Heart Falls in Love with Visions of Perfection (6/15/90 – 6/2/91)
Like When You Wave at a Train and the Train Hoots Back at You (Farid's Book) (6/11 – 7/26/91) (published by The Ecstatic Exchange, 2008)
Orpheus Meets Morpheus (8/1/91– 3/14/92)
The Puzzle (3/21/92 – 8/17/93)
The Greater Vehicle (10/17/93 – 4/30/94)
A Hundred Little 3-D Pictures (5/14/94 – 9/11/95)
The Angel Broadcast (9/29 – 12/17/95)
Mecca/Medina Time-Warp (12/19/95 – 1/6/96) (published as a Zilzal Press chapbook, 1996) (published in Sparrow on the Prophet's Tomb, The Ecstatic Exchange, 2010)
Miracle Songs for the Millennium (1/20 – 10/16/96)
The Blind Beekeeper (11/15/96 – 5/30/97) (published 2002 by Jusoor/Syracuse University Press)
Chants for the Beauty Feast (6/3 – 10/28/97) (published by The Ecstatic Exchange, 2011)
You Open a Door and it's a Starry Night (10/29/97 – 5/23/98) (published by The Ecstatic Exchange, 2009)
Salt Prayers (5/29 – 10/24/98) (published by The Ecstatic Exchange, 2005)
Some (10/25/98 – 4/25/99)
Flight to Egypt (5/1 – 5/16/99)
I Imagine a Lion (5/21 – 11/15/99) (published by The Ecstatic Exchange, 2006)
Millennial Prognostications (11/25/99 – 2/2/2000) (published by the Ecstatic Exchange, 2009)
Shaking the Quicksilver Pool (2/4 – 10/8/2000) (published by The Ecstatic Exchange, 2009)
Blood Songs (10/9/2000 – 4/3/2001)
The Music Space (4/10 – 9/16/2001) (published by The Ecstatic Exchange, 2007)

Where Death Goes (9/20/2001 – 5/1/2002) (published by The Ecstatic Exchange, 2009)

The Flame of Transformation Turns to Light (99 Ghazals Written in English) (5/14 – 8/21/2002) (published by The Ecstatic Exchange, 2007)

Through Rose-Colored Glasses (7/22/2002 – 1/15/2003) (published by The Ecstatic Exchange, 2007)

Psalms for the Broken-Hearted (1/22 – 5/25/2003) (published by The Ecstatic Exchange, 2006)

Hoopoe's Argument (5/27 – 9/18/03)

Love is a Letter Burning in a High Wind (9/21 – 11/6/2003) (published by The Ecstatic Exchange, 2006)

Laughing Buddha/Weeping Sufi (11/7/2003 – 1/10/2004) (published by The Ecstatic Exchange, 2005)

Mars and Beyond (1/20 – 3/29/2004) (published by The Ecstatic Exchange, 2005)

Underwater Galaxies (4/5 – 7/21/2004) (published by The Ecstatic Exchange, 2007)

Cooked Oranges (7/23/2004 – 1/24/2005 (published by The Ecstatic Exchange, 2007)

Holiday from the Perfect Crime (1/25 – 6/11/2005)

Stories Too Fiery to Sing Too Watery to Whisper (6/13 – 10/24/2005)

Coattails of the Saint (10/26/2005 – 5/10/2006) (published by The Ecstatic Exchange, 2006)

In the Realm of Neither (5/14/2006 – 11/12/06) (published by The Ecstatic Exchange, 2008)

Invention of the Wheel (11/13/06 – 6/10/07) (published by The Ecstatic Exchange, 2010)

The Sound of Geese Over the House (6/15 – 11/4/07)

The Fire Eater's Lunchbreak (11/11/07 – 5/19/2008) (published by The Ecstatic Exchange, 2008)

Sparks Off the Main Strike (5/24/2008 – 1/10/2009)(published by The Ecstatic Exchange, 2010)

Stretched Out on Amethysts (1/13 – 9/17/2009)(published by The Ecstatic Exchange, 2010)

The Throne Perpendicular to All that is Horizontal (9/18/09 – 1/25/10)

In Constant Incandescence (2/10 – 8/13/10)(published by The Ecstatic Exchange, 2011)

The Caged Bear Spies the Angel (8/30/10 –)

www.ingramcontent.com/pod-product-compliance
Lightning Source LLC
Chambersburg PA
CBHW020905090426
42736CB00008B/501